Presidio House

Colombian Slang for Brave Foreigners

National Edition

Presidio House LLC
2026

ISBN-13: 979-8-9951420-0-3

First Edition

Disclaimer

This book is a non-fiction educational and cultural guide to authentic colloquial Colombian Spanish. It contains real slang expressions used in everyday speech across different regions of Colombia, including informal, vulgar, strong, or regionally specific language that may be considered offensive, crude, or inappropriate in formal settings. All content is presented solely for linguistic, cultural, and educational purposes to help readers understand and communicate more naturally with native speakers.

The author and publisher do not endorse or encourage the use of profane, vulgar, or disrespectful language. Reader discretion is advised, especially for younger audiences or in professional/educational environments.

Welcome from La Vecina

¡Bienvenidos, valientes! Soy la Vecina de toda Colombia — esa amiga que te cuenta las vainas sin vueltas ni rodeos, como si ya estuviéramos tomando tinto en la esquina. Aquí empezamos con lo básico: cómo saludar como si ya fueras de la familia, cómo decir "sí" con estilo y cómo no meter la pata (ni dar papaya) al llegar. Este es el idioma que une a rolos, paisas, costeños y a todos los que vivimos en este país tan sabroso. Tú vas a sentirte en casa desde la primera frase, te lo prometo. ¡A darle con toda, que la vida es corta y las buenas historias no esperan!

English Welcome

Welcome, brave ones! I'm your national Vecina — that friend who spills the tea straight, no fluff, no nonsense. You know what I mean? We're kicking things off with the essentials: greetings that'll make you sound like you already belong to the family, ways to say "yes" with real style, and how not to give papaya the second you step off the plane. This is the Spanish that ties rolos, paisas, costeños, and everyone together in this delicious country. Grab a tinto, dive in, and you'll feel at home from the very first "¿qué más?" — life's too short not to sound like a local!

How to Use This Book

Each entry is set up the same way so you can jump in easily and start sounding local right away:

Phrase – the exact Colombian slang expression you're going to use

Vecina – that's me breaking it down in my warm, no-nonsense, street-smart voice

Meaning – the clear English meaning and the real vibe behind it

Example – a real-life sentence the way we actually say it on the street

Translation – the natural English version so you catch every bit of flavor

Go ahead and say them out loud, brave one. Slang isn't just words — it's flow, attitude, and that little sparkle you add when you drop it. ¡Pilas! You've got this.

Table of Contents

Saludos que te Hacen Sentir en Casa

Greetings That Make You Feel Like Family

(Entries 1–10)

Entry 1

¿Qué más pues, todo bien o qué?

Vecina:

Tú sueltas esto y ya estás hablando como de la familia — cálido, directo, y con ese cariño que los colombianos usamos cuando queremos que te sientas en casa desde el primer segundo.

Meaning:

Warm national greeting meaning "what's up, everything good?"

Example:

Oye parcero, ¿qué más pues, todo bien o qué? ¿Cómo va la vuelta?

Translation:

Hey buddy, what's up, everything good or what? How's everything going?

Entry 2

¿Qué hubo, qué se cuenta?

Vecina:

Este es el saludo que usas cuando ya hay confianza — como si le estuvieras preguntando al vecino que te vende tinto "¿qué ha pasado desde la última vez?".

Meaning:

Casual national greeting meaning "what's up, what's new?"

Example:

Parce, ¿qué hubo, qué se cuenta? Hace rato no te veo por aquí.

Translation:

Partner, what's up, what's new? Haven't seen you around in a while.

Entry 3

¿Todo en la buena o qué?

Vecina:

Cuando los colombianos preguntan esto, quieren saber que no hay drama — tú lo usas y ya suenas como uno más del grupo, sin tener que explicar nada.

Meaning:

Friendly national check-in meaning "everything going well, no drama?"

Example:

¿Todo en la buena o qué? Se te ve buena cara hoy, ¿qué pasó?

Translation:

Everything good or what? You look happy today, what happened?

Entry 4

¿Todo fluyendo o qué?

Vecina:

"Fluyendo" es la forma sabrosa de preguntar si la vida te está tratando bien — di esto y la gente te va a responder con una sonrisa porque saben que entiendes la vaina.

Meaning:

Chill national greeting meaning "everything flowing smoothly?"

Example: Hermano, ¿todo fluyendo o qué? La vaina va bien por allá?

Translation:

Bro, everything flowing okay? Things going good over there?

Entry 5

¿Qué dice la movida?

Vecina:

La “movida” es todo lo que está pasando a tu alrededor — tú lo preguntas y ya estás dentro del flow, como si hubieras estado ahí toda la vida.

Meaning:

Casual national greeting meaning “what’s the scene / what’s happening?”

Example:

¿Qué dice la movida por acá? ¿Hay plan esta noche?

Translation:

What’s the scene around here? Any plans tonight?

Entry 6

¿Todo bien por la casa?

Vecina:

Este es el saludo que usa la gente que de verdad se preocupa — tú lo dices y ya suenas como parte de la familia, preguntando por los pelaos y todo sin meterte en líos.

Meaning:

Warm national greeting meaning “everything good at home / with the family?”

Example:

Mami, ¿todo bien por la casa? ¿Los pelaos están juiciosos?

Translation:

Mom, everything good at home? The kids behaving?

Entry 7

¿Qué es la vuelta?

Vecina:

"La vuelta" es la forma colombiana de decir "cuéntame qué estás tramando" — úsalo y la gente te va a abrir el corazón porque saben que te interesa de verdad.

Meaning:

Informal national check-in meaning "what's the deal / what's up with you?"

Example:

Parce, ¿qué es la vuelta? Cuéntame qué estás tramando.

Translation:

Buddy, what's the deal? Tell me what you're up to.

Entry 8

¿Todo en la jugada o qué?

Vecina:

Cuando dices esto, estás diciendo "¿estás pilas o te dormiste?". Es el saludo que usan los que no se pierden de nada — y tú vas a sonar exactamente igual.

Meaning:

Casual national greeting meaning "you good / alert / in the game?"

Example:

¿Todo en la jugada o qué? No te duermas, que la cosa está buena.

Translation:

Everything good or what? Stay sharp, things are looking good.

Entry 9

¿Cómo va la vuelta?

Vecina:

Otra forma sabrosa de preguntar cómo van las cosas — tú lo usas y la gente te va a contar todo porque suena natural, como si ya fueras de aquí.

Meaning:

Warm national greeting meaning "how are things going / how's it rolling?"

Example:

¿Cómo va la vuelta, mi gente? ¿Todo fluyendo o hay lío?

Translation:

How's it going, my people? Everything flowing or is there drama?

Entry 10 ¿Todo en la buena vibra?

Vecina:

“Buena vibra” es esa energía linda que todos buscamos — tú lo preguntas y ya estás invitando a la otra persona a que te cuente lo bueno, porque aquí la vida se vive con sabor.

Meaning:

Friendly national check meaning “everything good vibes / positive energy?”

Example:

¿Todo en la buena vibra? Se siente rico el ambiente hoy.

Translation:

Everything good vibes? The energy feels nice today.

Aprobación con Sabor Colombiano

Approval with Real Colombian Flavor

(Entries 11–20)

Entry 11

De una, sin mente

Vecina:

Tú dices "de una" y ya estás dentro — sin pensarlo dos veces, con toda la actitud colombiana que dice "vamos pa'lante".

Meaning:

Right away, instantly, without hesitation

Example:

¿Vas o no? De una, sin mente, yo me le mido.

Translation:

You in or not? Right away, no overthinking — I'm down.

Entry 12

Hágale que eso es breve

Vecina:

Este es el empujoncito que damos cuando algo es rápido y fácil — tú lo usas y la gente te va a seguir porque suena práctico y sabroso.

Meaning:

Do it — it's quick and easy, no big deal

Example:

Hágale que eso es breve, yo voy y vuelvo en cinco minutos.

Translation:

Just do it, it's quick — I'll be back in five minutes.

Entry 13

Eso está una chimba

Vecina:

Cuando algo te encanta de verdad, "una chimba" es la forma más colombiana de decirlo — tú lo sueltas y la gente te va a responder con una sonrisa grande.

Meaning:

That's awesome / excellent / top-tier great

Example:

Ese parche que armaron está una chimba, pura buena vibra.

Translation:

That hangout you guys set up is awesome, pure good energy.

Entry 14

Va con toda esa vuelta

Vecina:

Esto es cuando alguien se mete de lleno sin guardar nada — tú lo dices y ya estás reconociendo que la persona va con toda la actitud colombiana.

Meaning:

Going all in / full commitment with attitude

Example:

Va con toda esa vuelta, no se guarda nada, ese man es serio.

Translation:

He's going all in, no holding back — that guy is serious.

Entry 15

Me le mido sin miedo

Vecina:

Cuando tú dices esto, estás mostrando que no te tiembla la mano — puro valor colombiano, y la gente te va a respetar por eso.

Meaning:

I'm jumping in confidently, no fear

Example:

Me le mido sin miedo, si hay que hablar, yo hablo.

Translation:

I'm stepping up without fear — if we need to talk, I'll talk.

Entry 16

Eso está melísimo

Vecina:

“Melísimo” es esa palabra cariñosa que usamos cuando algo está más que bueno — tú lo dices y ya estás invitando a que todo el mundo lo pruebe.

Meaning:

That’s really nice / delicious / awesome

Example:

El plan que armaste está melísimo, vamos a gozar.

Translation:

The plan you made is really nice — we’re going to have fun.

Entry 17

De una pa’ lo que sea

Vecina:

Esto es disposición total, sin condiciones tú lo sueltas y la gente sabe que contigo siempre se puede contar, pase lo que pase.

Meaning:

I’m in 100% / down for whatever, no conditions

Example:

De una pa’ lo que sea, tú sabes que conmigo cuentas.

Translation:

Down for whatever — you know you can count on me.

Entry 18

Eso pinta sabroso

Vecina:

Cuando algo promete mucho, "pinta sabroso" es la forma más rica de decirlo — tú lo usas y ya estás creando expectativa buena.

Meaning:

That looks promising / tasty / really good **Example:** Ese negocio pinta sabroso, hay que meterle ficha.

Translation:

That deal looks promising — we need to put effort in.

Entry 19

Eso va fino

Vecina:

"Va fino" es cuando todo está fluyendo elegante y sin problemas — tú lo dices y la gente sabe que estás aprobando con clase.

Meaning:

That's going smooth / sharp / well done

Example:

El proyecto va fino, todo cuadrado y sin problemas.

Translation:

The project is going smoothly — everything organized and no issues.

Entry 20

Eso está en la jugada

Vecina:

Cuando algo ya está activo y listo, "en la jugada" es la forma colombiana de decirlo — tú lo usas y ya estás dentro del parche.

Meaning:

That's in play / on point / ready and active

Example:

El parche está en la jugada, ya hay gente llegando.

Translation:

The hangout is on — people are already showing up.

Emoción que se Siente en el Alma

Emotions That Hit You in the Soul

(Entries 21–30)

Entry 21

Estoy que exploto

Vecina:

Tú dices esto cuando la emoción ya no cabe en el pecho — es pura explosión colombiana, como cuando te llega una noticia buena y no puedes guardártela.

Meaning:

I'm about to burst / exploding with excitement

Example:

Estoy que exploto con esta noticia, ¡no lo puedo creer!

Translation:

I'm bursting with this news — I can't believe it!

Entry 22

Me tiene volando

Vecina:

Cuando algo te pone feliz de verdad, "me tiene volando" es la forma más sabrosa de decirlo — tú lo sueltas y la gente sabe que estás en las nubes.

Meaning:

It's got me flying / super happy / on cloud nine

Example:

Esa canción me tiene volando, pura buena energía.

Translation:

That song has me flying — pure good energy.

Entry 23

Estoy en otra dimensión

Vecina:

Esto es cuando el momento es tan bueno que ya no estás en el mismo mundo — tú lo dices y todo el mundo entiende que estás viviendo algo especial.

Meaning:

I’m in another dimension / on another level

Example:

Con este parche estoy en otra dimensión, qué chimba.

Translation:

With this hangout I’m on another level — so awesome.

Entry 24

Me dejó viendo estrellas

Vecina:

Cuando algo te impacta fuerte y te deja sin palabras, “me dejó viendo estrellas” es la expresión perfecta tú la usas y ya estás contando que te voló la cabeza.

Meaning:

That blew my mind / left me seeing stars

Example:

El gol que metió me dejó viendo estrellas, ¡qué locura!

Translation:

That goal he scored blew my mind — what a crazy moment!

Entry 25

Estoy embalado mal

Vecina:

"Embalado mal" es cuando estás metido full en algo y no paras ni para comer — tú lo dices y la gente sabe que vas con todo el corazón.

Meaning:

I'm fully locked in / deep into it

Example:

Estoy embalado mal con este proyecto, no paro ni pa' comer.

Translation:

I'm deep into this project — I don't even stop to eat.

Entry 26

Me tiene alborotado

Vecina:

Cuando algo te tiene emocionado y sin poder quedarte quieto, "me tiene alborotado" es la forma más colombiana de explicarlo — tú lo sueltas y ya se nota la energía.

Meaning:

It's got me all stirred up / excited and restless **Example:**

El concierto me tiene alborotado, no puedo esperar.

Translation:

The concert has me all worked up — I can't wait.

Entry 27

Estoy prendido duro

Vecina:

Esto es cuando tienes la energía por las nubes y listo para todo — tú lo dices y la gente sabe que esa noche nadie te para.

Meaning:

I'm fired up hard / super energized

Example:

Estoy prendido duro pa' la rumba de esta noche.

Translation:

I'm super fired up for tonight's party.

Entry 28

Me voló la cabeza feo

Vecina:

Cuando algo te sorprende tanto que te deja loco, "me voló la cabeza feo" es la expresión que usamos para decir que fue heavy — tú la sueltas y ya estás contando la historia.

Meaning:

That blew my mind hard

Example:

La sorpresa que me dieron me voló la cabeza feo.

Translation:

The surprise they gave me completely blew my mind.

Entry 29

Estoy en mi salsa

Vecina:

Cuando estás en tu elemento y todo fluye natural, “estoy en mi salsa” es la forma más sabrosa de decirlo — tú lo usas y la gente sabe que nadie te para.

Meaning:

I’m in my element / in my zone

Example:

Cuando bailo salsa estoy en mi salsa, nadie me para.

Translation:

When I dance salsa I’m in my element — no one can stop me.

Entry 30

Me tiene eléctrico

Vecina:

Cuando la energía te recorre entero y no quieres que termine, “me tiene eléctrico” es la forma más viva de contarlo — tú lo dices y ya se siente la chispa.

Meaning:

It’s got me electric / buzzing with intensity

Example:

Esta energía me tiene eléctrico, no me quiero ir nunca.

Translation:

This energy has me buzzing — I never want to leave.

Fiesta y Rumba Sabrosa

Fiesta and Tasty Rumba Vibes

(Entries 31–40)

Entry 31

Se armó el mierdero

Vecina:

When the crew shows up and everything goes beautifully out of control, "se armó el mierdero" is how we say the real party has exploded — you'll feel the energy the second you drop it.

Meaning:

Things got wild / the crazy fun chaos started **Example:** Llegaron los pelaos y se armó el mierdero, qué rico. **Translation:**

The crew arrived and things got wild — so much fun.

Entry 32

Esto está prendido en candela

Vecina:

When the rumba is burning hot and nobody wants to leave, "prendido en candela" is the way we say the party is on fire — you'll sound like you've been dancing all night. **Meaning:**

This is lit / on fire / burning hot party

Example:

La rumba está prendida en candela, nadie se quiere ir.

Translation:

The party is on fire — no one wants to leave.

Entry 33

Se puso sabroso esto

Vecina:

When the vibe turns really good after a couple of drinks, “se puso sabroso esto” is how we say the night just got tasty — you’ll hear it everywhere once the music hits.

Meaning:

This got really good / enjoyable

Example:

Después del segundo trago se puso sabroso esto.

Translation:

After the second drink this got really good.

Entry 34

Esto está que arde

Vecina:

When the dance floor or the party hits its peak, “esto está que arde” is the perfect line — you’ll sound like a local the moment the heat rises.

Meaning:

This is peaking / on fire / maximum intensity **Example:**
La pista está que arde, todos bailando sin parar.
Translation:

The dance floor is on fire — everyone dancing non-stop.

Entry 35

Se formó la rumba dura

Vecina:

When the real non-stop party kicks off, "se formó la rumba dura" is how we announce it — you'll feel the difference the second you say it.

Meaning:

The real party started / non-stop rager

Example:

Se formó la rumba dura, esto va hasta las seis de la mañana.

Translation:

The real party kicked off — this goes until 6 a.m.

Entry 36

Esto está descontrolado

Vecina:

When the fun has no rules and everyone is just enjoying, "esto está descontrolado" is the joyful way we say it's out of control — pure Colombian party energy.

Meaning:

This is out of control / pure fun chaos

Example:

Con esa música esto está descontrolado, ¡qué gozo!

Translation:

With that music this is out of control — what a blast!

Entry 37

Se prendió la vuelta

Vecina:

When the vibe suddenly catches fire and nobody wants to go home, "se prendió la vuelta" is the line that tells everyone the night is alive — you'll love saying it.

Meaning:

The vibe caught fire / party's fully on now

Example:

Llegó el DJ y se prendió la vuelta, nadie se va.

Translation:

The DJ arrived and the vibe caught fire — no one's leaving.

Entry 38

Esto está a otro nivel

Vecina:

When the party or the moment jumps to the next level, "esto está a otro nivel" is how we say it's major league now — you'll sound like you belong.

Meaning:

This is next level / major league now

Example:

Con estos pelaos esto está a otro nivel, qué chimba.

Translation:

With this crew this is next level — so awesome.

Entry 39

Aquí fue donde fue

Vecina:

When you hit the exact moment the party peaked, "aquí fue donde fue" is the perfect way to point it out — you'll be the one everyone remembers saying it.

Meaning:

That's where it all went down / peaked

Example:

Aquí fue donde fue, cuando empezó el reguetón pesado.

Translation:

That's where it all happened — when the heavy reggaetón started.

Entry 40

Esto está que no cabe un alma

Vecina:

When the place is packed to the brim with good people, "esto está que no cabe un alma" is how we say it's full — you'll feel the excitement the moment you walk in.

Meaning:

It's packed / standing room only

Example:

El bar está que no cabe un alma, pura gente buena.

Translation:

The bar is packed to the brim — full of good people.

Dinero y la Vaina de la Plata

Money and the Whole Money Thing
(Entries 41–50)

Entry 41

Estoy en la inmunda

Vecina:

When you're completely broke and can't even afford a tinto, "estoy en la inmunda" is the funny way we say we have zero pesos — you'll hear it a lot at the end of the month.

Meaning:

I'm completely broke / dirt poor

Example:

Estoy en la inmunda, ni pa'l tinto me alcanza hoy.

Translation:

I'm flat broke — can't even afford a coffee today.

Entry 42

No tengo ni pa' un tinto

Vecina:

This is the classic line when your pockets are so empty you can't buy even the smallest coffee — you'll sound 100 % Colombian the moment you say it.

Meaning:

Don't even have money for a coffee / totally broke

Example:

No tengo ni pa' un tinto, estoy pelado mal.

Translation:

Not even enough for a coffee — I'm seriously broke.

Entry 43

Quedé viendo un chispero

Vecina:

When you end up with nothing after spending everything, "quedé viendo un chispero" is the humorous way we say we're left staring at empty hands.

Meaning:

Left with nothing / empty-handed

Example:

Después del paseo quedé viendo un chispero, sin un peso.

Translation:

After the trip I was left with nothing — not a single peso.

Entry 44

Estoy pelado mal Vecina:

"Pelado mal" is when you're seriously broke and have to tighten the belt — you'll use this one and everyone will nod because they've been there.

Meaning:

I'm flat broke / seriously broke

Example:

Estoy pelado mal, toca apretarme el cinturón este mes.

Translation:

I'm flat broke — gotta tighten the belt this month.

Entry 45 No hay con qué hacer la vuelta Vecina: When you literally have no money to make any moves, "no hay con qué hacer la vuelta" is the straightforward way we say everything is on hold. **Meaning:** No money to make moves / can't even get around **Example:** No hay con qué hacer la vuelta, estoy seco total. **Translation:** No money to do anything — I'm completely dry.

Entry 46 Estoy sin un peso encima Vecina: This is the honest line when you don't have a single peso in your pocket — you'll say it and people will laugh because they know exactly how it feels. **Meaning:** I don't have a single peso on me / zero cash **Example:** Estoy sin un peso encima, ni pa'l bus tengo. **Translation:** I don't have a single peso — not even bus fare.

Entry 47 La plata se me fue volando

Vecina:

When the money disappears faster than you expected, “la plata se me fue volando” is the perfect way to say it flew away — you’ll hear this one every weekend.

Meaning:

The money disappeared super fast

Example:

La plata se me fue volando en el fin de semana, qué salado.

Translation:

The money flew away over the weekend — what bad luck.

Entry 48

Ando más seco que un desierto

Vecina:

When your wallet is bone-dry, “ando más seco que un desierto” is the funny comparison we use — you’ll get smiles every time you drop it.

Meaning:

I’m drier than the desert / bone dry, no money

Example:

Ando más seco que un desierto, no tengo ni pa’l almuerzo.

Translation:

I’m drier than the desert — don’t even have money for lunch.

Entry 49

No tengo ni pa' moverme

Vecina:

This is when you can't even afford to move from where you are — you'll use it and everyone will understand you're completely stuck.

Meaning:

Can't even afford to move / no money at all

Example:

No tengo ni pa' moverme, estoy en la inmunda total.

Translation:

Can't even afford to get around — I'm completely broke.

Entry 50

Estoy quebrado hoy

Vecina:

When you're broke just for today but tomorrow looks better, "estoy quebrado hoy" is the hopeful way we say it — you'll sound real and optimistic at the same time.

Meaning:

I'm broke today / financially broken for now

Example:

Estoy quebrado hoy, pero mañana llega la plata.

Translation: I'm broke today — but the money comes tomorrow.

La Vecina Says

Carácter Colombiano de Verdad

Real Colombian Character

(Entries 51–60)

Entry 51 Ese man es una fiera

Vecina:

When someone is tough and doesn't back down, "ese man es una fiera" is how we say he's a beast — you'll use this and everyone will know exactly the kind of person you're talking about.

Meaning:

That guy is a beast / tough as hell

Example:

Ese man es una fiera negociando, no le bajan el precio.

Translation:

That guy is a beast at negotiating — they can't lower his price.

Entry 52

No se le arruga a nadie

Vecina:

This is the highest compliment we give someone who never flinches — you drop this line and people will instantly respect the person you're describing.

Meaning:

Doesn't back down from anyone / fearless

Example:

Ese parce no se le arruga a nadie, siempre responde.

Translation:

That partner doesn't back down from anyone — always steps up.

Entry 53

Tiene calle ese man

Vecina:

When someone really knows how the world works, "tiene calle" is our way of saying he's got real street smarts — you'll sound like a true Colombian when you use it.

Meaning:

That guy has street smarts / real world experience

Example:

Tiene calle ese man, sabe cómo manejarse en cualquier lado.

Translation:

That guy has street smarts — knows how to handle himself anywhere.

Entry 54

Se para firme donde sea

Vecina:

This is when someone stands their ground no matter where they are — you say it and everyone knows they're solid, no matter the situation.

Meaning:

Stands firm anywhere / doesn't flinch

Example:

Se para firme donde sea, no le tiembla la voz.

Translation:

He stands firm anywhere — his voice never shakes.

Entry 55

Es de los que no copia

Vecina:

When someone has their own unique style and never copies anyone, "es de los que no copia" is the perfect way to praise them — you'll use this and people will smile because it's true.

Meaning:

Doesn't copy others / has his own original style

Example:

Es de los que no copia, siempre tiene su flow propio.

Translation:

He's one who doesn't copy — always has his own flow.

Entry 56

No come de cuento

Vecina:

This is for the sharp ones who never fall for nonsense — you say it and everyone knows the person stays alert and doesn't get played.

Meaning:

Doesn't fall for bs / stays alert

Example:

Ese no come de cuento, siempre está pilas con todo.

Translation:

He doesn't fall for nonsense — always stays sharp.

Entry 57

Tiene más mundo que muchos

Vecina:

When someone has seen and lived a lot, "tiene más mundo que muchos" is how we say they're way more experienced — you'll sound wise when you use it.

Meaning:

Has seen more of the world / way more experienced

Example:

Tiene más mundo que muchos, sabe cómo es la cosa.

Translation:

He's seen more of the world than most — he knows how it works.

Entry 58

No le baja la mirada a nadie

Vecina:

This is pure confidence — when someone never lowers their gaze, you say this and everyone understands they're solid and fearless.

Meaning:

Doesn't lower his gaze to anyone / confident as hell

Example:

No le baja la mirada a nadie, siempre firme.

Translation:

He doesn't lower his gaze to anyone — always solid.

Entry 59

Es de los que responde duro

Vecina:

When someone steps up strong when it matters, "es de los que responde duro" is the way we praise them — you'll use this and people will nod with respect.

Meaning:

Steps up hard when needed / delivers strongly

Example:

Es de los que responde duro cuando la cosa se pone fea.

Translation:

He's one who steps up hard when things get tough.

Entry 60

No se deja montar

Vecina:

This is for the ones who never let anyone push them around — you say it and everyone knows they set their own boundaries with class.

Meaning:

Doesn't let anyone push him around

Example:

Ese man no se deja montar, siempre pone los puntos.

Translation:

That guy doesn't let anyone push him around — always sets boundaries.

Estado de Ánimo y Buena Vibra

Mood and Good Vibes

(Entries 61–70)

Entry 61

Estoy vuelto nada

Vecina:

When the day has drained every last bit of energy and you feel like nothing is left, "estoy vuelto nada" is how we say we're completely wiped — you'll use this and everyone will nod because they've been there.

Meaning:

I'm completely drained / turned into nothing

Example:

Después del trabajo estoy vuelto nada, necesito descansar.

Translation:

After work I'm completely drained — I need to rest.

Entry 62

Quedé hecho polvo

Vecina:

After a long rumba or a heavy week, "quedé hecho polvo" is the perfect way to say you're totally wiped out — you'll sound real and relatable the moment you drop it.

Meaning:

Left exhausted / wiped out

Example:

Después de la rumba quedé hecho polvo, no puedo ni moverme.

Translation:

After the party I was wiped out — can't even move.

Entry 63

Estoy que no doy más

Vecina:

When you've reached your absolute limit and can't go any further, "estoy que no doy más" is how we admit we're done — you'll say it and people will understand without you explaining.

Meaning:

I can't go on / at my limit

Example:

Estoy que no doy más, esta semana fue muy pesada.

Translation:

I can't go on — this week was too heavy.

Entry 64

Me dejó fundido

Vecina:

When something (a trip, work, or even a good party) leaves you with zero battery, "me dejó fundido" is the way we say we're burnt out — you'll use this and everyone will offer you a tinto.

Meaning:

Left me burnt out / no battery left

Example:

El viaje me dejó fundido, necesito dormir dos días.

Translation:

The trip left me burnt out — I need to sleep for two days.

Entry 65

Estoy en la mala dura

Vecina:

When everything seems to go wrong in one day, "estoy en la mala dura" is how we describe a really rough streak — you'll say it and people will laugh because they know the feeling.

Meaning:

Having a really rough day / bad streak

Example:

Hoy estoy en la mala dura, todo me sale al revés.

Translation:

Today I'm having a really rough time — everything's going wrong.

Entry 66

Ando vuelto mierda

Vecina:

When things have gone completely sideways and you feel like crap, "ando vuelto mierda" is the raw way we say it — you'll use this and friends will know exactly how to cheer you up.

Meaning:

Everything went wrong / feeling like crap

Example:

Ando vuelto mierda después de esa discusión.

Translation:

I'm feeling like crap after that argument.

Entry 67

Estoy tranquilo hoy

Vecina:

When your body and mind finally line up and everything feels calm, "estoy tranquilo hoy" is the peaceful way we say it — you'll drop this and people will smile because it's a good day.

Meaning:

Calm today / body and mind aligned

Example:

Hoy estoy tranquilo, todo fluye sin afán.

Translation: Today I'm calm — everything flowing without rush.

Entry 68

Todo va en calma

Vecina:

When there's no drama and life is flowing smoothly inside, "todo va en calma" is how we describe that inner peace — you'll say it and everyone will feel the good vibe.

Meaning:

Everything going calmly / inner peace

Example:

Todo va en calma, no hay drama por aquí.

Translation:

Everything's calm — no drama around here.

Entry 69

Estoy relajado

Vecina:

When you're truly relaxed and the day feels easy, "estoy relajado" is the simple way we say it — you'll use this while sitting with a tinto and people will know you're in a good place.

Meaning:

I'm relaxed / like still water

Example:

Estoy relajado, tomando un tinto en la plaza.

Translation:

I'm relaxed — having a coffee in the plaza.

Entry 70

Todo fluye bonito

Vecina:

When life is moving nicely with good company and no obstacles, "todo fluye bonito" is the sweetest way we describe it — you'll say it and everyone will agree that today feels right.

Meaning:

Everything flows nicely / smoothly

Example:

Con buena compañía todo fluye bonito, qué rico.

Translation:

With good company everything flows nicely — so nice.

Cultura que Une a Todo el País

Culture That Unites the Country

(Entries 71–80)

Entry 71

Aquí todo es con sabor

Vecina:

When you're in Colombia you quickly learn that everything — even the calmest moments — comes with flavor, you'll feel that swing the second you step into any corner of the country.

Meaning:

Everything here has flavor / even calm has swing

Example:

Aquí todo es con sabor, hasta un café sabe diferente.

Translation:

Everything here has flavor — even a coffee tastes different.

Entry 72

Aquí la vida es tranquila

Vecina:

Here life moves at a peaceful pace but never gets boring — you'll notice how that calm actually feels alive once you slow down and breathe with us.

Meaning:

Life here is peaceful / but alive

Example:

Aquí la vida es tranquila, pero nunca aburrida.

Translation:

Life here is peaceful — but never boring.

Entry 73

Esto es pura alegría

Vecina:

This is pure joy — steady and warm, not loud — you'll feel it in the music playing from every balcony and the way people smile without needing a reason.

Meaning:

This is pure joy / steady and unflashy

Example:

Este barrio es pura alegría, siempre hay música.

Translation:

This neighborhood is pure joy — there's always music.

Entry 74

Aquí la gente es querida

Vecina:

Here people are truly loved and that love holds everything together — you'll see it when a stranger helps you without being asked.

Meaning:

Here people are beloved / that holds everything together

Example:

Aquí la gente es querida, todos se ayudan.

Translation:

Here people are loved — everyone helps each other.

Entry 75

Esto es de pura sabrosura

Vecina:

This is pure tastiness — not just the food but the whole way we live — you'll taste it in every plate and every conversation.

Meaning:

Pure tastiness / flavorful way of life

Example:

La comida colombiana es de pura sabrosura, ¿no?

Translation:

Colombian food is pure deliciousness, right?

Entry 76

Aquí todo se goza

Vecina:

Here we enjoy everything — even the simple things like a rainy afternoon — you'll start doing the same once you let the rhythm catch you.

Meaning:

Everything is enjoyed here / even the simple things

Example:

Aquí todo se goza, hasta un día de lluvia.

Translation:

Here everything is enjoyed — even a rainy day.

Entry 77

Esto es ritmo y corazón

Vecina:

This is rhythm and heart — that's what defines us you'll feel both beating stronger the longer you stay.

Meaning:

Rhythm and heart / that defines a lot here

Example:

Colombia es ritmo y corazón, pura pasión.

Translation:

Colombia is rhythm and heart — pure passion.

Entry 78

Aquí todo tiene su tumbao

Vecina:

Here everything has its own rhythmic swagger — even the way people walk — you'll catch that tumbao yourself after a few days with us.

Meaning:

Everything has its tumbao / rhythmic swagger

Example:

Aquí todo tiene su tumbao, hasta caminar.

Translation:

Everything here has swagger — even walking.

Entry 79

Esto es vida sabrosa

Vecina:

This is tasty life — not perfect, but lived fully — you'll start understanding that once you stop rushing and just enjoy the flavor.

Meaning:

Tasty life / well-lived even if not perfect

Example:

Esto es vida sabrosa, con sus altos y bajos.

Translation:

This is a tasty life — with its ups and downs.

Entry 80

Aquí todo se vive bonito

Vecina:

Here everything is lived beautifully — with love and flavor — you'll feel it in your bones and never want to leave the same way you arrived.

Meaning:

Everything is lived beautifully / understood here

Example:

Aquí todo se vive bonito, con cariño y sabor.

Translation:

Here everything is lived beautifully — with love and flavor.

Representative Glossary

(CS-01 National Edition)

Chimba
Vecina: The word we throw around when something is straight-up awesome — you'll catch yourself saying it after your first real Colombian experience.
Meaning: Awesome / great

Papaya
Vecina: Vulnerability / easy target — the thing you never want to "give" because it leaves you wide open, so watch out!
Meaning: Vulnerability / easy target

Parce
Vecina: Our favorite way to call someone a buddy or partner — drop this and you instantly sound like you belong to the crew.
Meaning: Buddy / partner

Pila

Vecina: Sharp / alert — the quality we admire most, because in Colombia you have to stay "pila" to keep up with the flow.

Meaning: Sharp / alert

Bacano

Vecina: Cool / great — the relaxed way we say something or someone is genuinely good, you'll hear it all day long.

Meaning: Cool / great

Rumba

Vecina: Party — the word that turns any night into an adventure, because for us a rumba is never just a party, it's a vibe.

Meaning: Party

Vaina

Vecina: Thing / stuff — our all-purpose word for any situation, plan, or problem; once you start using "vaina" you'll feel very Colombian.

Meaning: Thing / stuff

De una Vecina:
Right away — the fastest way to say “I’m in” with zero hesitation, pure Colombian energy.
Meaning: Right away

Sabroso
Vecina: Tasty / enjoyable — we use this for food, music, moments, and life itself; everything here should feel sabroso.
Meaning: Tasty / enjoyable

Buena vibra
Vecina: Good energy / positive vibe — the feeling we chase in every gathering; you’ll start noticing it the moment you relax and join in.
Meaning: Good energy / positive vibe

Discover the Collection

La Vecina Says

The 8-Volume Series

Here's the full collection so you can keep exploring every corner of Colombia:

CS-01 – Colombian Slang for Brave Foreigners

CS-02 – Paisa Slang for Brave Foreigners

CS-03 – Rolo Slang for Brave Foreigners

CS-04 – Caleño Slang for Brave Foreigners

CS-05 – Cafetero Slang for Brave Foreigners

CS-06 – Costeño Slang for Brave Foreigners

CS-07 – Santandereano & Boyacense Slang for Brave Foreigners

CS-08 – Pacific Coast Slang for Brave Foreigners

Acknowledgements

Vecina:

Gracias de corazón a todos los colombianos que mantienen vivo este idioma tan vivo y sabroso. Sin ustedes, nada de esto tendría sabor. Y a ti, valiente lector, gracias por atreverte a aprender con nosotros. ¡Nos vemos en la próxima vuelta!

www.ingramcontent.com/pod-product-compliance
Lightning Source LLC
LaVergne TN
LVHW011052110826
845149LV00015B/3463

* 9 7 9 8 9 9 5 1 4 2 0 0 3 *